Other books written or edited by the author:

The Dictionary of Philosophy
Letters to My Son
Letters to My Daughter
Of God, the Devil and the Jews
The Soviet Impact on Society
Twentieth Century Philosophy
On the Nature of Man
Treasury of Philosophy
Spinoza Dictionary
Spinoza's Road to Inner Freedom
The Hebrew Impact on Society
The Talmud of Jerusalem
Wisdom of the Torah

A Book
of
Contemplation

by

Dagobert D. Runes

PHILOSOPHICAL LIBRARY

New York

Omnia praeclara
tam difficilia quam
rara sunt

BARUCH SPINOZA

Alles Vergängliche ist
nur ein Gleichnis

JOHANN WOLFGANG V. GÖTHE

A WORD TO THE READER

The thoughts expressed in this small book, unrelated as they appear, are bound together by a humble but dogged search for what is true in nature and what is good in man.

It is as difficult to think through the prejudices and traditional concepts of one's own time as it is easy to bemuse one's self with those of the past generations; and should I have displeased or offended any person or group, I am most eager to state that I intend to hurt no one but the enemies of a kindlier Today and a better Tomorrow.

D. D. R.

A BOOK OF
CONTEMPLATION

A

ABNORMAL: All great ideas and all great actors on the stage of history were abnormal. Was Beethoven normal? Or Michelangelo? Da Vinci, Socrates, or Mohammed?

They all went off the norm, driving themselves incessantly for what they thought was vital and essential. You may call them neurotics, if you wish. Surely their response to given impulses was undue, strikingly undue, in the eyes of living mediocrities.

The nights of the truly outstanding are inhabited by demons, idols and visions. But without their fantasies and dreams, a dull place the normal era would be.

ABNORMALITY: Treat gently the abnormal; he may carry some subtle talent under the cloud of his peculiarities.

ABOLITIONISM: The white man took willingly the black man as burden, but hesitates to take him as friend.

ABSENCE increases fondness—and ends in forgetfulness.

THE ABSOLUTE: As far as morals are concerned, what matters is only our awareness that they are relative to time, place and government.

ADHERENCE: Preconceived notions are the hardest to give up.

ADMIRATION: Who fails to admire will never love.

ADOLESCENCE: Neither infancy nor childhood, but adolescence is decisive in the making of man. The tastes, physical and mental, fostered in those days will determine the rest of the living years.

ADVERSITY is God's helpmate and the Devil's handmaiden.

ADVICE should be given by the example of the accomplished, not by one's own meager experience.

AGE: Man's true age lies in the life span ahead of him, not the span behind him.

❋

Age is no cause for veneration. An old

[4]

crocodile is still a menace and an old crow sings not like a nightingale.

*

Age is wasted on the tired. It is the most precious time of life.

*

Wisdom grows with the years but not in a barren soul.

*

Gray hair is a sign of age, not wisdom.

AGNOSTIC: A timid person attempting to hide his insecurity under a metaphysical cloak. He is gnostic about himself but agnostic about everything else.

AGGRESSION: How quick the sand of life runs out, and even the wasting is made doleful by man's impatient eristics.

AHIMSA: This, the Hindu principle of non-killing of cows and other animals, has led to the killing of hundreds of thousands of Indian Moslems who ignored it. How often a religious tenet so drifts away from the original spirit that it leads to its opposite.

ALCOHOLISM: Society's legitimatized drug addiction.

ALMS were the early expression of social consciousness. The man who refused alms then is the cynic of our era.

AMATEUR: It is by the quality of his mistakes that you recognize the amateur.

AMBITION: Great ambition has sometimes destroyed the one it possessed, but raised mankind a step or two.

AMERICA was erected with material that the builders had rejected: adventurers, refugees, criminals, bonded persons, slaves, the hunted and the outcasts. Its glory is the nimbus that forever hazes about the down-trodden.

*

America has freed the world and the world can not forgive her for that.

ANCESTOR WORSHIP may not only lead youth to search amid their heritage for the lasting values, but may tend to make older people prove their virtues by today's deeds.

ANGELS are in the heavens, I am sure, because there are deeds done by mortals that are difficult to explain by the mortal nature of man. The angels of self-sacrifice and everlasting devotion, of courage and tenderness—they

[6]

must be fluttering about in the winds high above, sometimes taking on the face of man and his flesh.

*

Why did the Lord make so few winged ones and so many that crawl?

*

I don't know if the angels have wings; I am sure the devils do, they move about so fast.

ANIMALS have no conscience. If they did, they would be better than people.

*

Animals we all are, but they live for today, we for a tomorrow.

APOLOGY: People will apologize for stepping on each other's toes, but not for crushing each other's hearts.

APPLAUSE: Some can handle it and are stimulated—others just get drunk.

APPROVAL by a fool is worse than rejection by a sage.

ARGUMENT: The philosophical mind never wishes to win an argument, but rather the truth.

[7]

Argument is a sure sign of conversation gone sour.

*

Some argue to prove a point, others to prove themselves.

ARISTOCRACY: Leaning on ancestors proves most often that aristocracy hardly ever outlasts its first generations.

*

A horse does not become a thoroughbred by chewing its oats without snorting, nor a man by genteel handling of knife and fork.

*

What was good in aristocracies is long disappeared and what is left is good for nothing.

*

There are no old families. Some got at the moneybag sooner, that's all.

ARROGANCE will create, in the strong, distaste; in the weaklings, admiration. What a weak era we live in!

*

A racehorse strut ill becomes a donkey.

ART: Dilettantes interpret art for art's sake as art for the artist's sake.

[8]

Art for art's sake is like cake for cake's sake. It has to please someone or it is just a ragout of ingredients.

*

Genius may be novel but novelties are not genius.

ATHEISTS are often enough shamefaced antitheists. They wish no *Theos,* no God, no Principle to interfere with the petty advantages of their little existences. Their penny needs are the sole currency accepted.

ATTITUDE: To a goat the most delicate garden is just a grazing place.

AUTHOR: It is imagination that makes a writer, not schooling, and you can't teach the first.

AUTOBIOGRAPHY may be history, if offered forthright; biography is mostly fiction, be it glib or ardent.

B

BABES: The Bible says you get the truth from them. Perhaps—if you get to them before they learn the ways of man.

BEAUTY is only tinsel if it makes you not better, happier.

*

Beauty travels on many levels. There is a beauty seen by the heart, one seen by the mind, and one by the guts and sex glands. A steak can be beautiful and so can an architectural plan. I even heard a physician exclaim: "What a beautiful eczema!"

BIBLE: It is an odd book—the word of God, rituals of priests, legends, dull chronicles, and a sprinkling of childish lore—still, this poorly edited anthology has outlasted all the master epics. A book is just a bit of literature but the Bible is the very vessel of *Shechinah*, the spirit of man, between heaven and earth.

It is an unfinished book. Who dares to say that Israel has yielded its last prophet?

❀

If the Book is not worth living by, it is not worth pretending by.

❀

Let God speak through the Book and bid the priests be silent.

❀

If the good Lord did not write the Bible, then King Solomon did, with some help from his father, David.

BIG MEN have the same problems as little ones, but on a greater scale.

BIOGRAPHIES are rarely worth reading. They are written by either flatterers or antagonists. At best they only give you the neighbors' opinion of the hero, or some imagined composite put together with clippings and transcripts. We often don't know what really motivates the soul of our nearest kin or acquaintance. Who dares to state with any degree of certainty what moved a man a century ago, a thousand miles away?

The biographer is like the man who longs to see the legendary lady in the castle window. She raises the blinds only when she is ready for you, all made up and dressed up and smiled up. From afar, you can scarcely tell whether she is 17 or 70, and when you take a second look the blinds come down.

BODY CHEMISTRY: Its influence upon mental structure is sharply emphasized in the sudden change of attitude in man and woman right after the culmination of the sexual act.

BOOK: Our libraries are getting bigger, which makes it more difficult to find a good book. The shelves are groaning under the pressure of clothbound nothingness.

❋

A book is great by what you give to it, not take from it.

❋

The truly great book does not find its readers, it creates them.

❋

You may never find a friend but you can always find a book. And with books as your

[12]

friends, you will not go through life a lonely man.

*

Big books are like overgrown people—fine to stare at but little else.

*

Books are the invisible tie between the people of the world. The Torah binds the Jews as the Qoran the Moslems and the Gospels the Christian nations. Confucius bound the Chinese and so did Lao-tse and Buddha; until books were replaced by Marx' *Capital*.

The gods live in the books and where the books disappeared, the gods went with them. Gone are the Carthaginians, the Sumerians, and all their minor deities that never had a book of their own.

Books are all we have of the gods of the past, and of the present as well. And so the Book remains with us the ever-heritage of the tie with the heavens. Take away the books and you have a turmoil of people without unity or direction.

[13]

Books are so long because the writers sell the harvest before they separate the wheat from the chaff.

BRAINPOWER: Only a fraction of mankind's mental capacity is being used. The overwhelming bulk of the world's brainpower perishes unused because of totalitarian executions or war activities, because of a stunted literacy of skill among seven-tenths of the population, and finally because of premature assignment to dulling labor. We are running the world on one cylinder instead of ten.

BROTHERHOOD: Who is not his brother's keeper belongs not to the family of man.

*

Be wary of the protagonist for brotherhood of mankind; likely as not, he pleads for love in terms of abstract billions of unknown foreigners because he never learned to love a small handful of his own people.

BUDDHISM in its essence rests on four great principles, those of kindness, pity, communal joy, and equanimity. Unlike Christendom, it managed to gain and retain loyal adherents without benefit of rack and faggot.

C

CABBALAH: The secret book of Hebrew tradition had no single author, nor had Torah nor Talmud. Its many authors wrote with sagacity which was not theirs but rather the reflection of the Divine Intellect they venerated.

*

The Cabbalah teaches that in the realm of cognition and inner being there are ten different spheres. Not even all those who speak for truth see it on the same level.

CAPITALISM: I would rather take capitalism without a soul than Communism without a heart.

CATHEDRAL: The most imposing cathedrals are never too far from slums.

CAUSALITY: There are two causes of every effect; the visible one, and the real one.

CHABAD: To understand the forces of the world

is not enough. To gain access to the creative powers, the Cabbalah teaches, one must have wisdom and intuition *(chochma* and *bina).* Only the three combined—*chochma, bina, da-at (chabad)*—raise man above the material world.

CHANGE: No man is the same for more than a fortnight.

CHARACTER: Suffering may not make character, but kindness will.

❉

Character must be seen in everyday life, not just in its Sunday best.

❉

Tell me what you read and I'll tell you what you are.

❉

It is when a man is in power that he shows his true direction and the measure of his patience.

CHARITY is not the effect of faith, it *is* faith.

❉

There is no charity so noble the cynic can not impugn its motivation.

CHILDREN perpetuate the prejudices and

superstitions of their parents, rarely their wisdom.

❋

The newborn starts off with a score of notches on which to hang the good things in life. Watch the community load him with prejudice, malice and superstition.

❋

— The wondrous adventures a child's mind can experience on a walk through a deserted, littered lot set between two old houses!

❋

Our ancestors called their newborn boy *Kaddish*, the Holy One. The child was their link to living eternity. Those who spend their existence without a child have no share in the fate of tomorrow's world. They circle around themselves with their backs to the future generations.

❋

To a child, its games of make-believe are as serious as our realities are to us. I sometimes wonder which of the two has more substance.

❋

There are no children, only young people.

CHRIST: The greatest number of books have been written about one whom we know the least: Jesus Christ. *WoW*

*

One cannot be a Christian while living the life of a pagan. If your heart is pagan and your deeds are pagan, you remain outside the Circle of Christ, which means Church of Christ, no matter what prayers your lips speak, nor what the ikon before which you genuflect.

*

The Jews always have denied and forever will oppose the concept of God besides God. God is *Echod,* and One stands eternally for no more and no less, no picture of Him, no son of Him. This philosophy unendingly separates Judaism from Christianity.

*

If He came to earth today, He would never forgive us, in all His celestial beatitude, for the unspeakable atrocities perpetrated on His kin and the kin of His mother and His faithful believers. All the paternosters and all the hymns of all fifty thousand saints and all fifty thousand theologians and all the genuflecting of a billion Christian knees, those alive today and those interred since the night of the catacombs, could not wear away the Jewish blood that is on Christian hands. If Jesus came to earth today, He would shrink from the Gothic cathedrals and the forest of church spires that carry the cross He took upon Himself that man might live a loving creature. Perhaps He would slink away to some little ghetto street in New York City, where there is a tiny ten-by-ten synagogue. And he would sit down with the other bearded Jews on the hard benches in this true house of worship. And He would read with the others from the ancient book of Moses, which, as He said, He came to fulfill and not to destroy—the book of Moses, written in the script He could understand, written in the spirit in which He lived and for which He died.

*

God lived with the world and its people for a million years before Jesus was born, so why begin time with the Son of God? Why not with God, the Father? There must have been good and evil before Christ came to earth; there must have been sin and repentance, devotion and derision, helpfulness and viciousness, manliness and gentleness and godliness; there must have been saints and thieves, Falstaffs and ascetics, foul men and sound men, naive men and critics, the Lord's servants and the Devil's henchmen.

❋

There was a God before Jesus.

❋

It is easy to say, "I believe in God. I am a Christian." But is God in you? Is Jesus in you?

❋

Millions have died for Him, but only a few lived for Him.

❋

Jesus may have risen, but His followers stayed down.

CHURCHES have lost the touch of the Divine and turned to book reviews and politics.

CIVILIZATION can be judged by the value it places on human life.

❋

Civilization always looks to be at its peak to the present generation. I wonder what the ancients would say to our contemporary mass slaughters, torture and suppression.

CLASSICS: The devotion to classicism is given to most great men. It is their deep-felt urge to strengthen themselves on the ancient eras of heroism, virtue and faith.

CLEANLINESS is a consideration for others rather than oneself. For that reason, uncivilized people commonly are unclean.

CLEVERNESS will set the mind ajar; wisdom will set it at rest.

*

Cleverness is a poor substitute for understanding.

*

Cleverness is competitive, wisdom never.

COLOR: Man was made of clay. Clay is black or red, but never white. White man is a decadent creature, away from sun, wind, and the sea.

COMMUNISM is less a creed than an escape of the frustrated failure.

*

Communism has driven off the captains of

industry and replaced them with captains of demagogy.

*

Communism began by incarcerating the few to free the many, and then enchained the many to protect the few.

*

One of the great moral calamities perpetrated by the Communists is their having driven millions of persons to a flight into conformism, that is, phlegmatic acceptance of any and all directives coming from above without any wish for examination or criticism.

COMPANIONSHIP: No one can afford to go to hell in his own fashion; Hades admits sinners in pairs only.

COMPARISON: The great greeds are aroused by comparison. Free man endeavors to lead his life without comparison and thus without competition.

COMPASSION is the only one of the human emotions the Lord permitted Himself and it has carried the divine flavor ever since.

*

Those who do not feel injustice done to

others are not part of the play the Lord has been staging ever. They are mere walk-ons in the scenes of history.

COMPETITION: This would be a more tolerable world to live in if men would merely go about their tasks instead of trying to be better than fellow man.

COMRADE: Watch out for the Utopian magician—he has an axe up his sleeve.

COMRADESHIP: What some refer to as unity is often but a bond of common hatreds and prejudices.

CONCEIT   is the little man's substitute for self-satisfaction.

CONFESSION   of an old sin neither improves nor elevates man; the task lies in facing honestly your present failings and egocentricities.

CONFORMISM: In the land of the one-legged, the two-legged is a cripple.

*

Conforming with even an only suspected evil is the opportunist's choice of the easy path instead of the right one.

CONSCIENCE: Human conscience is the only true moral guide, since all so-called ethical precepts, as well as religious commands, may be—and have been—turned as easily to evil as to good.

❁

Conscience is not a soft pillow to sleep on but rather a bed of pangs and restlessness. Only the indolent can sleep when evil prowls in the night.

CONSTITUTION: Some of the worst tyrannies, such as those of Russia and China, have been built on the under-structure of an almost perfect constitution.

❁

A government is what it acts out, not what it pretends.

CONTROVERSY frequently divulges little about the issues at stake, but much about the motives of those disagreeing.

CONVERSATION: Fixed ideas are the roadblock on the path of discussion.

CONVERSION: The Jew who becomes a Christian or a Mohammedan or a Marxist because it admits him to a plush job in Vienna or

Moscow, is like the rice-Christian in China—
when the missionaries ran out of rice the
Chinese ran out of Christianity.

*

There is no need to drop Judaism for
Christianity. Jesus never left the Jewish fold,
but many times did the Christians desert
Jesus. God lives in the faith of man, not in
his churches.

*

If you don't find God in your own faith,
you will not find Him in a borrowed one.

CONVERTS: Torquemada and Hitler have made
more converts of Jews to Christianity than all
the missionaries of all times put together.
Only dread and the rack could make them
change the Star for a Cross and those who
changed have not made Jewry poorer nor
Christendom richer.

COSMOGONY: They speak of the Origin of the
Universe as if this tiny cosmos man sees were
the Lord's sole domain.

God lives in infinite mansions man can
neither see nor comprehend, and He is Being
in essence not to be fathomed or judged by
animal creatures.

Man hunts and searches on his whirling globe and whenever he unearths a miniature truth within his environ, he thinks himself close to the peak of science. But this very pinnacle itself is only a speck of dust on the infinite plain of God's realm.

COSMOS: Physically, we are a swiftly deteriorating fungus settled on a dust particle whirling rhythmically in a black and empty barrel —I say "empty" because the distances between one tiny planet and the other are so gigantic that they are little different from stray, hardly visible dust-bits in an "empty" container.

And yet this fungus, riding for fleeting seconds on the dust of space, thinks his barrel a universe—nay, *the universe*.

COURAGE   may sometimes be of doubtful issue, but cowardice never is.

*

Courage ennobles man. This is not a world of aristocrats.

*

It takes a few ribbons to make people die for their country. It takes much more to make them live for it.

COURTESY may be a veneer, but neither is rudeness the real thing.

CREATION: So difficult to conceive and yet more so to deny.

❋

Some want us to believe the whole solar system grew out of an idly floating gas bubble. Still, whence the bubble?

❋

The earth could not have been more dismal and dank before creation, when God moved on the face of the waters, than it is now. However, today through its formless bleakness runs a sanguine thread.

CRIME: There are no great criminals, only greatly misfortuned individuals. All crimes fit all people under altered circumstances.

❋

There is no crime so enormous that a better society could not have ameliorated it.

CRITIC: A skydreaming eagle without wings.

❋

He lacks the courage to write; the critic's box is safe.

CRUELTY is the coward's defense.

Although they know hunger and fear, dumb animals know no cruelty; it takes training to make man evil, snide, and cruel.

CURTAIN RAISERS: Four men who raised the curtain masking the heart of man: Solomon, Socrates, Shakespeare, Spinoza.

CYNIC means "dog" in Greek; the Greeks had the word for it.

❈

A cynic is worse than a fool. The fool lacks insight but has faith; the cynic lacks both, though his cloak of impudence covers this emptiness.

❈

A cynic cannot see from here to tomorrow.

D

THE DEAD: Let not the dead bury their dead; they might rise again.

DEATH: Perhaps our fear of death is but embryonic fear of life.

Death is a sideline guest who arrives and departs, but life comes to stay, with its thousand problems, difficulties, and obstacles. It is life that deserves our concern and our fears, not death.

❊

Some persons make such great efforts preparing themselves for life, as if they were to go on living for a thousand years. They are so busy getting ready that they hardly get to living.

❊

You have laughed God out of your schools, out of your books, and out of your life, but you can not laugh Him out of your death.

You still do your three score and ten, and then sink into dust knowing not the why and wherefore of this fleeting dream-trot in the arena of the human anthill.

❖

It matters less when we die than how much of our life will live on.

❖

Man sometimes lives, but constantly dies.

❖

The thought of Life seldom occurs but at the time of death.

❖

From the day of birth we never stop dying.

❖

The fool dies only once.

❖

It is not the fear of death that saddens people, but the love of life.

❖

While we dream we think we are being real; perhaps our reality is only a kind of dream, and death the awakening.

❖

Death is a solemn reminder that life should be lived, not spent.

❖

No man has nine lives but some die nine deaths.

Leave this world the way you found it: a heap of suffering and a drop of blessing. Don't run out without giving some of the latter—so many do.

DECEPTION: No one deceives us more often than we do ourselves.

DEEDS: If man is the image of God, then his deeds certainly belie his features.

*

Deeds only matter in the final analysis. Some nations gave their all to build up the body, like the Spartans; others to develop the mind, like the Athenians. The Judeans, however, cultivated the God-bound deed, *Mitzwah*, the act humane.

DEFEAT can be fate's kindest admonition.

DEMAGOGUE: The sanctimonious voice of righteousness is standard with the demagogue. No sincere man has as honest a face as the professional confidence man.

*

All tyrannical and demagogic undoings have their motivations. In fact in this motivation lies the root of the evil.

DEMIGODS: Judaism bars the crown of divinity from all and everything but the *Ruach Hakodesh*—the Holy Spirit that is the One Eternal, the *Echod*. It places the crown upon the Torah, the knowledge of God, the indwelling of God in man; God alone is King.

DEMOCRACY in its inherent toleration must be on guard against self-destruction.

DESPAIR is the mother of genius.

DEVIL: One may praise the Lord and serve the Devil.

*

The worst thing about the Devil is that most people flatly deny his existence. Obviously he can thus do considerable damage to body and soul without ever being blamed.

DIGNITY of the human person is the most meritorious aspect of democracy.

*

Dignity is a man-made respite of silence in a cacaphonic world of affront and fury.

DIPLOMACY is the verbal technique of saying what you don't mean and making it mean what you don't say.

*

Diplomacy is a game of make-believe with malice aforethought.

DISAPPOINTMENT is a signpost to true values.

DISCONTENT may become either spur or spite.

DISCRETION is the tact not to see what can't be helped.

DOCILITY is one of the major social crimes cultivated by the average man and woman. It is a crime because it contributes greatly to the domination by tyrannical individuals over the people at large. Docile submission to the prevailing set-up can scarcely be classified as anything but a criminal attitude.

DONOR: The greatest gift is the art of giving.

*

Those who give quietly, give twice.

DOUBLE LIFE: We all lead it, only it is usually more multiple.

DOUBLE LOYALTY is often challenged by those who have none.

DOUBT is also a creed.

*

It is amazing how some skeptics in one subject become gullible approaching another.

DREAMS: What mysteries do the Philistines expect to find in their dream life if their real
one is but commonplace?

DULLNESS   sets in when talk backtracks to the
surface.

E

ECONOMICS have hardly changed the people, but people have changed economy.

*

Man, so imperfect in body and mind, demands perfection of all things in his social and economic structure.

EDUCATION: God has been separated from our schools; that may be all right, but the Devil was left there and that is not fair. The Devil of prejudice, arrogance, hatred, envy, home-grown superstition, and success-greed hovers over the school benches. You can't exorcise the Devil by looking the other way.

*

Education in conscientious living will change the face of mankind; knowledge alone will only reshape the grimace.

*

The thinking of people usually depends

upon which side of their bread is buttered. This is especially true of the thinking done by the teaching profession in countries where the state administration does all the buttering.

❋

One need not be learned in the head to do the right thing, but rather learned in the heart. The learning of the heart is the most neglected branch of education today. The schools leave it to the churches and the churches leave it to the home, and how many homes are the proper place for character education?

❋

The heart can learn only from another heart. The printed word does not teach it.

❋

The system provides for instruction in almost any field excepting human conduct. In some schools they even teach you how to use a camera and how to collect stamps, but how to live a free man's life is left to latchkey parents and the older gang around the block. They have bolted the front gate against God and religion, but the Devil sneaks in through the back door.

EGOTISM: The most difficult person to make friends with is yourself.

ELECTIONS: Heads of government should be nominated by a committee of citizens, not elected by the masses passing judgment on the basis of the aspirants' rhetorical talents or demagogic trickery.

EMPATHY: Those who say they feel for all, likely feel only for one, their very own one.

ENCYCLOPEDISTS: Cumulative erudition is more appropriate on a shelf than in a man.

THE ENEMY: The character of mankind's foe changes from epoch to epoch. In earliest times anarchy was the great threat, the refusal of individual or tribe to respect the privileges of others. Pretentious usurpers were later the archfoe. Even religion for a while became a threat of suppressive organization. At present it is pretentious social welfare, sailing under the red flag of communism, threatening to engulf mankind with a tyrannical net spread by cunning demagogues.

ENVY: A man with mouse eyes can see little but the heels of another man.

Envy is the mother (forever denied) of much of the alleged love for humanity carried on the sleeves of political scoundrels.

EPIGONES often appropriate the laurels that should adorn the originator.

EQUALITY: All men are equal in sin, unequal in virtue.

EQUANIMITY is sometimes a symptom of indifference and not of mastered emotions.

ETHEREAL: Even into the darkest soul passes, at least once in life, a ray of awareness of the super-natural, sometimes at the birth of a child or the death of a soul. Like to those living in ancient Egypt's *Amenti,* the land of the dead, through which passed once a day the sun god, Ra.

ETHICS: People live on different wavelengths of time. Some live for the hour, others for the months or years, but few only for eternity. Long-range living is the way of true ethics.

*

If you failed to learn ethics at six, you will not learn it at sixty.

EVIL deeds are the crutches of little minds; they make them feel active and important.

[38]

There is so much misery and massacre in this world that to deny it one is either a fool or a faker.

EVOLUTION: If man is the royal crown of creation, I am an anarchist.

EXPERIENCE: If the dead were to rise and bury the living, I doubt if they'd make a better world. The only thing man seems to learn from experience is that it bears repetition. They killed the Czar to end tyranny, and began a free state with a new tyrant.

F

FACTS are difficult to accept because they must be grasped; mysteries are quickly taken on, since they require belief only.

FADDISTS use the reasoning of a scholar to prove a proposition little removed from old wives' fairy tales.

FAILURE: If you can do nothing with yourself, others are not likely to do better.

FAIRY TALES: The great tales were never written for the young. But our time has lost the spiritual naïveté of life, so only the children are left to respond to the simplicities of the ancient lore.

FAITH is nothing but knowledge that what we understand is only a shadow of the Unknown. Faith is the science of the pitiful limitations of man's mental scope.

*

Faith has its weaknesses, but faithlessness is the poorest substitute.

Adonai Echod! God is One, and the One lives in the heart of man, and the love to God and the love to man are one and the same. This is not only the beginning of true faith, this is all of it; the rest is silence.

❋

The man who has his own religion has a fool for a priest.

❋

Faith is belief in the invisible. It would be a dull world, indeed, if only the visible were reality.

❋

Faith and doubt are brothers under the skin.

❋

Faith is not proven by the number of believers. Abraham was alone and he had the truth against a whole generation of pagans.

FAME runs in circles. One can be burning with ambition within his little ring and be cold to the rest of the world.

❋

Fame spreads, elusive in the grasping arms of turbulent man until all the strength and

[41]

time and breath inherent to mortals are spent in the embrace of the clothed chimera, and man is left nothing but a stumbling shadow of his true self.

Fame cannot be possessed. It cannot even be arrested, and if some of the naïvely ambitious hold it for their own, let them take only one further look to find how precarious is their grip.

FANA-FIL-LAH: The Moslem saint's nirvana or annihilation in God is as little an ethical act as the ascetic seclusion of the Christian Trappist. An act exists as ethical or unethical only in relation to others. A flight into mystical hermitage may bring one peace or gratitude or forgetfulness but never is it a matter of morals. The saint is often more selfish than the sinner. Running away from the cares and battles of life may serve the interests of a burdened soul, but in the light of social morality it is just another deed strictly for the sake of the benefits it offers the doer.

FARMLIFE: Its idyllic aspects have been grossly overrated. The work of raising and tending kitchen requirements is hardly inspiring.

FASCISM: The path of the dictator is paved with democratic pronouncements.

FATALISM: The man who hates his enemies is no wiser than the child who hits at the chair over which he stumbled.

FATE: The unpredictable fall of events in our erratic stream of life. Sometimes what looks like a whirling trap to certain doom throws us onto a most attractive shore and what appears a stretch of gentle caressing waves will drag the unsuspecting to perdition. You can not tell what this goddess spins until the web is done and carried by the winds to the far-blue rocks of posterity.

FEAR: Who has the fear of God never had His love.

*

Fear is the severest of pains, and the least alleviated.

*

The unknown fears trouble us most.

*

Fear means nursing a problem instead of facing it. It is a play of self-pity ignoring the inevitable. It takes courage to brush aside broodings of temerity. Our sages said that the courageous die by the blade, the timid by a thousand strokes of their fears.

*

Those who endanger the safety of a state by their urge for power are prone to panic the people into fear of an imaginary enemy abroad.

FEARLESSNESS is shown not so much by those who stoically accept an inevitable verdict of death, but rather by those who could escape the death penalty if they would only submit.

FELLOWSHIP: You are what you arouse in fellow man.

FELLOW-TRAVELERS: They are so eager for perfection in social order that they accept chaos as a substitute provided it holds forth a promise for tomorrow.

FLAG: The American flag is a symbol, not of the nation, but of its freedom.

FLATTERY: He who flatters today will throw mud tomorrow.

*

Flattery is the first step on the road to slander.

[44]

Flattery is like an ill wind; it shifts without pause.

*

Men who tolerate flattery will never accept criticism.

*

Flattery is a scheme of the sly to bribe real people with make-believe currency.

FLIGHT: Man still has failed to gain the secrets of muscle-powered bird flight although he has mastered the winds; just as he has conquered the waters by use of the boat, but not learned to swim like the fish.

FLOWERS: Petals that light up a feeling of beauty in one nation are just feed in another.

FOE: There is no better friend than a frank enemy.

FOOLS are not those who know little but rather those who know too much of what just isn't so.

*

Men are fools, but not so much as those who think themselves exceptions to this dictum.

FORCE   has made slaves of men but it is justice that makes men of slaves.

FOREIGN LANGUAGE: With the number of platitudes and irrelevancies being spouted by mouth and pen in any one language, the acquisition of additional tongues should be soundly discouraged.

FORGETTING: The art of forgetting is as important as that of remembering.

FORGIVENESS: The infant and the dying show the look of forgivenesss—Eternity smiling at man's pitiful self-importance in coming and going.

❀

Forgiveness is a decision no longer to see the evil; forgetfulness is understanding it as a part of the chain of woe.

❀

Can you forgive the snake its poisonous fangs, the tarantula its sting, the leopard its claws? Such is man to man.

❀

If it's divine to forgive, it's manly to forget.

FORTUNE   has no rhyme or reason, like the rock that falls on an anthill. Perhaps the surviving ants think they were saved by divine providence and send up hymns of thanks.

*

Fortune, more than rarely, is great misfortune.

FREEDOM: Free men have no right to live and work in isolation if they wish to retain the bliss of their heritage. Rather is it their duty to crash into the lairs of the slave-makers and slave-holders, so that the rest of the world may become free and stay free.

*

Freedom lies not in the resignation to want, but rather in the accession to true values.

*

Freedom is not dominant where subjugation still exists, even in a corner.

*

Freedom knows only pro and contra with no neutrality in between, only cowardice or opportunism.

FRIEND: Wheat does not come without chaff. If you want your friend, accept his entourage.

FRIENDSHIP: Too often are close relationships founded on dislike and envy called friendships, for we are bound to those we hate almost as much as to those we love. Perhaps hatred is even a stronger tie than affection; it is more lasting, and like love, seeks out its object, yearning to dwell in its shadow.

*

Like the Stone of Wisdom, friendship may be lying right in your backyard and you may never know it.

*

Those who cannot give friendship will rarely receive it and never hold it.

*

Your friend is the one who sees you as you would love to see yourself.

*

Friendship is a daydream beat of the heart for a face that lights it up. Only in dreams can one see in that simple trifle all virtues, valiance and varied attributes that warm the clasp of the hands. In the light of friendship, the commonplace fades into a serene glow and banality metamorphoses a romance. What touching reality in such dreams, and how barren existence in mere objective togetherness!

*

Meet with your friends in the core of the

matter, where you agree, and not on the fringe where you differ.

FUTURE: The best way to look ahead is by looking back.

*

If you understand your past, the future will hold no riddles.

G

GAB: Some gabble with the tongue, others with the pen.

Every sinner was punished by the good Lord with a handicap: the dullard got the gift of gab.

GENIUS is no part of madness, but madmen may have genius.

GENEROSITY: To find fault in our heart is easy; to find generosity in it is difficult.

GIFTS: He who gives too much belittles the recipient.

GLORY: The sweet smell of military victory has, like all perfumes, a very putrid matter as base.

GOD: The essence of all Being is One, and there our wisdom ends. But this we feel and know as well as we, with our little souls, can grasp the thought: the way to God is man's love to man.

*

The soul of God is in the soul of man. There is no God but in the consciousness of innermost man.

*

God has no interpreters but man's hearkening, and the church may or may not speak His voice. The voice of God is too high for some to hear and too low for others, and it does not exist at all for the many, many who are deaf. The voice of God may speak through the morning green of a sun-kissed meadow, the melancholy rhymes of bittersweet poetry, the angry shouts of a dying soldier giving his life on the battlefield altar of freedom, the years of parental drudgery and filial sacrifice, heavenly sermons and songs leaving the lips of the truly inspired, the words of wisdom of sages then and now.

*

There is no God besides the God in the depths of man's mind. There is no love and inner freedom but that springs from the fountain of truly divine cognition. There is no unity but the everlasting truth borne by man's inner self.

✳

Man lived without God for a million years. He now dwells in the presence of God, but does God dwell in the heart of man?

✳

The ancient Hebrews did not write the name of God. I often wish the Christians would follow suit, as never was a word more misused in writing and speaking than the name of the Lord.

✳

If modern man understands the Ways of the Lord, then the Master is in a bad way.

✳

The small mind envisions a smallish God and then denies Him. One has to be a big man to see God in His glory, a very big man indeed.

✳

The Hebrews have no name for Him, the Moslems have a hundred. Both suggest the same thing, that there are concepts as well as emotions that can be communicated only allegorically.

God is poor company for those who don't speak His language.

*

God moves in deepest silence over the sands, the oceans and the sod. Only the thirsty soul will spy His footprints.

*

God is a silent partner in this world, and man certainly gives Him the short end.

*

If He intended to fashion man in His image, He certainly was interrupted on the job.

GODHEAD: To get nearer to God, come closer to man.

GOLDEN MEAN: Those who follow the golden middle way often have a profound appreciation of the value of gold.

GOLDEN RULE: Do to others as you say you do.

GOOD CHEER is not virtue but a step toward it. Baal Shem Tov, the Hebrew saint, said: I can sing a prayer as well as say it.

GOOD TIMES: Some people bear up worse under good times than under bad.

GRADING: That we have great men in our time and olden times is not because of our educational system, but rather in spite of it. They are the ones the teachers couldn't spoil. At least they couldn't spoil them altogether, although some important figures of our times bear the mark of moral confusion and anti-social behavior. Some of them use their gifts and talents to sing the praise of totalitarian dictators. Others do not hesitate to undermine and betray the welfare of the democratic community they live in.

How can it be otherwise in a society in which the teachers have not yet learned that youth raised in ambition, self-assertion and competitive avarice will not grow into charitable adulthood. And if some think that they can beat more knowledge into youth by the scourge of the contest than by mere teaching, I would say that an ounce of human kindness is worth a ton of so-called knowledge. It isn't that you need the scourge to train the youth, just as it isn't the whip you need to keep man at work. Give man a proper job and a proper wage and freedom to live in, and he will stay at a task until it is done, because man is made to work. And give a child answers to his curious mind in open manner and in proper time, and give him freedom to query and freedom to participate in equal manner with all his classmates without fear of being degraded, without bribe of rank promises, and the child will follow your teaching eagerly, because youth wants to learn.

Does a father grade his children? Does he mark them low and high, passing and failing? They are his to teach and love alike. And if some lack the color of speech or the power of persuasion to entertain the interests of the young, perhaps they should seek for other fields of work instead of holding school over a herd of uneasy scholars, and leave teaching to those who feel the calling and have the cordiality of the teaching mind.

GRAMMAR: The best grammarian still can't write a verse.

＊

Grammarians make no new thoughts, but thoughts make new grammar.

GRATITUDE: People who set out to hurt you will, in the long run, help you as often as those who desire to be of assistance may harm you.

*

Gratitude forever faces the obstacle of envy.

GREAT IDEAS were never discovered by one man, but often stopped by one.

GREAT MEN are sometimes very small men.

GREATNESS: Great men are simple—but what intricate simplicity!

GREAT THOUGHTS ever walk the open road. Pretenses seek out the misty byways.

GRIEF can only be cured by reason, and reason rests with God.

*

Those who do not care easily master their grief.

GUILT: Man is equal to any crime or sin under given circumstances. Those whom fate spared or favored are inclined to condemn in haste the one who drew a bad lot.

*

Guilt by association is not conclusive, but

considerable. I think little of the virgin who spends her days in a brothel.

Some of the most unspeakable crimes leave telling marks but no telling evidence.

*

Lack of punishment is no proof of innocence.

H

HACHUKKIM: Some of the laws of the Torah can not be rationally justified. Perhaps some of them had only one purpose, to make all the people of the country do the same thing at the same time with the same devotion— a practice in discipline and religion, a training in unity and obedience to higher principles.

HAPPINESS: Perhaps hogs are happy, but man should be moved by a greater wish than to be jolly.

*

Happiness is not a virtue, but virtue brings happiness.

*

Happiness is determined by the number of people one loves.

*

Happiness is a task, not a gift.

HASTE: Those who run through life will get

there quickly, but hardly well-composed.

HATE: Dictators long ago found out it is easier to unite people in common hatred than in common love.

*

Hate binds no less than love. The free man will want to put it behind him. Hatred disfigures your words no less than your lips.

*

One who hates an evildoer fails to recognize that those with ill will, more often than not, serve us instead of their own interests.

*

One may avoid, confine or punish a culprit without snarling. To love an enemy, however, is absurd; it is difficult enough to love one's friends.

*

Whatever you love, you are its master; whatever you hate, you are its slave.

*

Hate ignores the wise truth that all evildoers are such by necessity. They do need be curbed, like thorns or thistles, but hate is unwarranted in weeding.

HEART is the mind's bridge to wisdom.

HEAVEN: The Cabbalah speaks of ten steps to heaven. There is modesty, and courage, and devotion, and so on. The book never mentions libido as a rung to beatitude.

HELP: The man who needs no one's help is a lonely man indeed.

HERITAGE: You can tell a thousand years later when a great man left his imprint on the mind of a nation.

HERMIT: The hermit is a dull man preoccupied with nothing but his little self, be it physical, be it spiritual. The wise man, like Socrates, seeks out the people of the world and makes them part of his own self, the greater Self of the greater man.

HEROES: True honor does not crave recognition, as true wisdom craves not publicity. The great heroes and the great men of wisdom walk silently through the bypaths of mankind.

*

Some of those buried in prison yards deserved mausoleums, and many of those entombed in cathedral sepulchers should have been thrown to the jackals. The tombstone tells when you died, not how you lived.

HEROISM: The man who will risk his life on a childish dare may not do the same if the welfare of a whole nation hangs on it.

HERO WORSHIP has an uncanny tendency to choose scoundrels as the object of adulation.

HISTORY: Frequently in history the burden rested on men behind the screen; the fancy and proud actors on the stage were only marionettes.

❋

History of our global events is merely an insignificant whisper on the fringe of the titanic battles of the cosmos, our blood- and tear-soaked earth but a splinter falling in the aeonic conflicts to a brief span of rest.

❋

Of the lives of the oppressors in history there should be only one brief note identifying their tenebrous existence; the rest of it, with castle, equestrian statue, fancy dress with crown and mace and bloody sword, ought to go into a black book filled with hearty tales and pitiful songs. Social un-

[61]

derstanding, searching for the life and work and suffering of the little people whose memory seems all but buried beneath the showy tinsel of the people's malefactors.

❊

There are too few books from the pen of those who made history and too many by those who poorly retraced it.

❊

Every historian writes as if his little country were the center of the globe—and nothing can convince him otherwise.

❊

History should be taught backwards. It makes for a more sombre panorama. We did not climb from rags to riches. We still fight for waterways and island rights like growling cavemen, we grovel before arrogant overlords and sneer and hiss at men of other color.

❊

History is a planless sequence of little events and situations. Had England remained a peninsula, as it was not so long ago, Napoleon might have conquered all of Europe and the British Empire perhaps would never have come to be.

If the Czar had executed Lenin instead of imprisoning him, Russia likely would have stayed a liberal socialist country under Kerenski.

If the Babylonian Jews had come to the rescue of beleaguered Jerusalem in the year 70 instead of defaulting on their promise of asssistance, Judea would perhaps have lived on, and its people would not have been dispersed. Vespasian had no more Roman armies to spare.

A thousand little things—a poorly directed dagger or bullet, a geographical oddity, a quirk of circumstance—and the world would have taken a different shape.

*

History has three sides to it: the wrong side, the right side, and the way it really happened.

*

Glory is the most precious gift posterity can bestow upon its deserving ancestors. It is one measure which even the most powerful of potentates can neither falsify nor escape. If there is any glory to the Imperium Romanum, it lies in the ruins of the temples

which they destroyed, not in the gory epics
of their conquests and victories. I do not wish
to know the ugly details of how the mer-
cenary legions vanquished neighbor after
neighbor. I do not want to know the sinister
data of their evil hierarchy that began with
Romulus and ran its sanguine course through
the Western world for a thousand years and
more. I say it matters little what Caesar be-
fouled his own mother and what Messalina
put womanhood to shame. Furthermore, I
would say that all that type of history is not
a history of the people, but rather of its ex-
ploiters, its usurpers, its false prophets.

The wars of conquest by self-appointed or
family-perpetuated masters over an enslaved
people are not the history of the world, but
rather the story of man's iniquity and unspeakable cruelty to fellow man. The hard-
ships and tortures with which usurpers and
their ilk terrorized mankind are a terrible,
but only a single, chapter in the great book
of the story of man, to be read like the verse
on Purgatory as a reminder and a lesson. The
story of man begins where the chapter of
tyranny ends and he who embellishes the

misdeeds of the blackguards, be they ancient or of recent vintage, teaches not history but the perversion of it.

Come forth, the man to tell the story of the little people, people that till the earth and raise the fruit, that fish in the ocean and lakes and rivers and hunt in the forests and breed the stock and trade in the markets and make a thousand things of use or of pleasure for man and child. Come forth, the man to tell the story of these people, the real people, those that work and those that pray, those that wander and sing and play and lead the good life and have fellowship in their hearts and sincerity in their hands.

These are the people who deserve the glory that posterity can bestow. Their world should be written about. How they fared and how they failed should be related in the books of history, and not, certainly not, all that plush and plunder, that weird twosome of tournament and dungeon that signifies the era of courtly tyranny blighting mankind like the plague it was.

*

There are as many versions of history as

there are nations, and then some.

HOBBY is a man's endeavor to make an avocation give him the satisfaction an occupation should.

HOME is where your friends are.

HOMILETICS: I wish they would remember that Moses was a poor speaker, still his was the voice of God.

HONESTY: The confidence man has honesty always on his lips.

HONOR and dignity are matters of cognition, not recognition.

HOSTILITY begins at home. If school does not eradicate it, life has little chance.

HUMBLENESS before a principle is the measure of a man's faith and character.

HUMILITY: It takes a lot of thought to fathom human knowledge, and rare intellectual humility to realize that the greatest depth of man's thinking still runs only in shallow grooves.

HUMOR is the harbinger of persuasion; lack of it foretells discord.

A sense of humor is sense for sure.

*

Humor is the daughter of reason; she makes game of self-important pretentiousness.

HUNGER   is the father of servility.

IDEALISM: Idealism is an approach to life, not an end in itself. One can be quite materialistic about so-called ideal things, such as religion, literature and the arts. On the other hand, one can be quite idealistic about material things, such as the living conditions of the working or farming man.

IDEAS: Words, profound and meaningless, pop out when thought fails.

*

More people have died for false idols than true ideas.

IDLENESS is preoccupation with the barnacles of thought.

IDOLS: If it be true that one becomes like what he worships, what monsters this world's idols must be!

IGNORANCE: Most people don't care enough

to search for the facts of the issues they talk about with such concern.

IMAGINATION: Reality—what a poor substitute for imagination!

＊

Imagination is the arena of the genius.

＊

Science, too, must ride Pegasus—diligence its legs, but imagination its wings.

＊

Heaven is a matter of imagination but so is hate, love, and pretty much everything else.

IMITATION is nine-tenths of our cultural pattern.

IMMORALITY: Acts of animalism are nothing more than that; immoral they are not. Immorality occurs only when there exists an antagonistic tendency or act against society.

IMMORTALITY is no more fabulous than birth: that out of dust and dirt can rise an organism of a billion muscles, nerves and bones, to talk and walk and think and then dry up and bury itself back into a hole of dirt and dust. Who can fathom the whereto and wherefore of life immortal?

In passing away we only take to the heavens what we leave to mankind.

INDEPENDENCE is the wish of a peasant: to raise porridge with his own two hands.

❊

The free man wants to live, create and work in interdependence. Man is to man a Devil but also a God.

INDIFFERENCE: Being wrong is no disgrace, being indifferent is.

AN INFIDEL is one who does not accept the superstitions of his community.

INHIBITIONS: It isn't the lack of inhibitions that distinguishes man from man but rather the choice of inhibitions. The lack of inhibitions merely distinguishes animal from man.

INSANITY is a frequent visitor of genius under stress, a strange guest of the lonely in their flight from reality.

❊

The insane mind has as many variations as the sane; sometimes I wonder which one contributes more to the madness of the world.

❊

For the very same actions and expressions

some were declared to be suffering from religious mania, others were called saints and divines.

INTEGRITY: They teach you early how to wash your face and body, in school and home, but how to cleanse your mind of putrid ideas and prejudice, that is left unsaid and thus undone. I am afraid that even the occasional ablutions in the church are scarcely purifying, no more than face-saving. They walk about with shining faces and decaying souls.

INTERESTING: Even the dullest is interesting when speaking his mind honestly; it is the scintillating surface conversationalist who is the intolerable bore.

INTUITION is thinking ahead, as reason is thinking back.

ISSUES: Handle people with gloves, but issues, bare-fisted.

J

JAILS: Stables designed to improve ethics by herding together the sinners. As sin will always come out on top, the result of this process is invariably the acquisition of at least one new sin by the old sinners.

You cannot make a man straight by having him live a crooked jail-life.

JEST   is but honeyed criticism.

JEW: What blasphemy is the theology of crucifixion—to paint the Jews as the destroyer of religion when the Jew is really its creator!

*

Jews have been stunted in their growth by a hostile world from the days of Israel, the God fighter. They were chosen by the Lord to carry the Tablets of the Law, but their neighbors wanted them to carry the cross, or the banner of the crescent.

They decimated the chosen ones, decade

after decade, century after century, with forced conversion, rack and pyre and noxious gases, and what could have been by now a nation of a hundred million children of Israel, is left a poor tenth after two millennia without grace and charity.

*

Many attribute to the Jews their own failing and then hate them for it.

*

Jews are the heart-people of our era. Could you see Jesus as a German, Frenchman or Chinese? Or Paul as a Japanese or Scotchman?

JUDAISM has no sects, only attributes. What does it matter where one meets God and His Beatitude, be it in one great principle or in numerous precepts and legends?

*

Judaism is the story of a great father popularized by two difficult offsprings.

JUDGMENT: Listening to both sides does not necessarily bring about a correct judgment.

JURY: An untrained group of balance-keepers upholding the truth hidden between shady lawyers.

JUSTICE is more a question of attitude than fact.

*

Stand on the side of the weaker and you'll always be on the right side.

*

Justice is a poor substitute for compassion.

*

Justice is like a greased pig: many touch it, few hold on to it.

K

KEENNESS: It takes a rough stone to sharpen the edge.

KERA: They all have it, *Kera*. The Cabbalists refer to it as one eye on the realms of glittering everyday values. Few are the star-eyed with only one Lord, one aim, and one love.

KINSHIP: A man after my own heart means a man with my own prejudices.

KLAN: Jesus never stopped in Georgia but Lucifer did.

KNOWLEDGE: It takes a lot of knowledge to understand how little we know.

❀

Learn what you know and not what's alien. Can the worm in the stomach see the light of the moon?

We think in the light of our planetary group of rocks, which we euphemistically call "the universe." This is as little the Universe as man's stomach, although the latter may appear as the world of worlds to a worm or germ.

All conjectures beyond our firmaments of space and thought are theological dream-spinning and no more, fantasies of one fungus on a speck of dust talking to another on the nature of powers beyond.

❊

There is no knowledge—only a lesser state of ignorance.

❊

Knowledge *may* be good; kindness is good.

❊

Knowledge dwells in three mansions: the house of words, the home of facts, and the niche of wisdom. It is the last only that harbors peace of mind.

❊

Only the ignorant know everything.

❊

Some are satisfied when they hear it, some when they see it, and others stop when they have a Greek word for it; only too few go beyond the word.

L

LABOR: The laborer is not a better man than the capitalist, only less fortunate.

*

Tyranny of labor is no better than tyranny of military or industry.

LANGUAGE makes not the man; it is the man who makes language. Perhaps our schools would do better to guide the young in a search for the truer thought, the deeper concept, instead of a better syntax.

LAST WORDS: May your last words be like your first: a cry for the nearness of loved ones.

LAUGHTER brings tears into your eyes. It is the twin sister of weeping; oftentimes they are so close together, you wonder which way to turn.

LAW is as varied as the sentiments of those who rule.

A law is as proper as the motives of the ruler.

❋

The law is never holy but often sinful. And perhaps even today, in this freest of countries of all times and places, there may be many who stand on the wrong side of the law, placed thus not because they went astray, but rather because the law strayed from the right path.

It is the lawbreakers in our history who have brought to the people of the Western world the rights they enjoy, and if the enchained East is to come to its freedom, it will again be the lawbreakers who will tumble the overbearing colossus of legitimate totalitarianism.

❋

The law is the crime it purports to prevent.

❋

It is with the breaking of the law that the freedom of man began; the bills of rights were written with the blood of heretics and lawbreakers.

LAYMEN: We are all laymen, only some more so than others.

[78]

LEARNING: Speak to your own self and let it teach you.

*

Honor is a poor reward for the pleasures of study. Where honor is set as the price of education, the mind may pack in many facts and data in its hasty reach for the goal, but the heart will become forbidding and corrupted.

*

Education must serve a purpose or it may fall into a wrong one. Tradition had a grip on the school as a parcel of princely property, and to use such property on behalf of the crown was the scope of tradition. Such scope is unchanged in the lands which are vassals to totalitarian masters, where the youth is no more than a chunk of state property manipulated, like all of life, limb and holdings, for the benefit of a demagogic clique. But in the free lands, youth is not a means but a goal, each person to be respected as a body and mind in his own right, to be dealt with not in competition and tasteless comparison.

In our free society we aim to treat the porter with the same regard as the pundit, the janitor like the judge, the pauper like the millionaire. Upon such equality our social organization is based, and in such equality our youth is to be raised. The poor in memory, the poor in perception, the slow in thinking and the weak in diligence are to be handled with the very same attitude as those enriched in all respects.

A child can as little help being lesser mentally as it can help being so physically. There is as little fairness in catering to the gifted and setting back the deprived as there is in constantly praising the beauties of a pretty child and noting the defects, scars and pimples of a homely one.

LEISURE is the dream-time of doing nothing spun by the many who stay on the wrong job.

*

The great hunt of the masses: to kill time.

LIE: Some would search and twist to come to truth, while others do the same to protect a lie.

LIFE is a rather short walk through eternity. Be they seeds, pups or infants, on the trek all

[80]

pick up weight, sensitivity and awareness.
Then, much before the end of the run,
they deteriorate, head, legs, and lungs. The
tragicomedy of existence: the long walk of
slow decay.

*

It is not how old you are that matters, but
how many hours of your life you have lived.

*

Man creative lives many lives; some men
are so dull they do not live even once.

*

Life is so crowded with everyday, it takes
great effort to step aside and just watch and
think.

*

Few only live their own life; so many have
it lived by others.

LISTENING: The most precious thing a man
can lend is his ears.

LITERATURE: There are confidence men in
literature as well as in finance, business and
politics.

*

The worst thing that ever happened to

writing is that it became a business. The purpose of business is to make money, and to achieve that end it is necessary to please as many people as possible, to amuse them, to entertain them—in short, to do everything that will help increase the volume of sales.

*

A book occurs when man experiences things of great depth and significance and feels compelled to relate his inner experiences. There are such books, written ones as well as unwritten ones.

*

If only those would write who have something to say, many who should only watch would get off the field.

LIVE   as you want to be remembered.

LONELINESS   is rare and peculiar company.

LONGEVITY: Even the fleeting butterfly has an infancy, adolescence, middle age and senescence. Perhaps a select few live a bit beyond their three score and ten hours.

LOVE: If only man would stop loving humanity and deity and begin to love just himself—not that in himself which is on the lowest level of

man, but rather that in himself which oc-
cupies the highest rung.

*

The word "love" belongs in that small
group of general terms that is used more frequently to disguise an intent or a thought
than to divulge it. And if "love" is used in
combination with "humanity," the word becomes the most dangerous befogger of them
all.

*

To love people is to know them.

*

There is a lover even for a crab.

*

Love is the passion of grief. Amid all the
sunlight of affection, there falls the shadow
of life rushing away.

*

All men love themselves, but some also
hate the rest of the world.

*

Hate comes naturally, love is to be learned.

*

Love may be so ethereal that the presence
of the beloved may reduce the state rather
than increase it. Still, love is no more than
the wish to be together.

Love is the desire to be together, and no more. Whoever sends his beloved away has long ceased to love, no matter how reluctant he may be to admit it. Sometimes nostalgic tremors may linger on after the beat of love has been stilled.

❋

There are some words that need to be broken up, such as "love." There should be different terms for the lust to mate and for man's heartful devotion to kin, friend, or God.

When Messalina seduced a new slave into her bedroom, she called it love; when King David heard of the death of Jonathan, he cried out, "I loved thee more than this earth understands"; when a lecherous roué marries his latest child-bride, he quakes, "I love you"; when the prophet Isaiah fell under the dagger of the assassin, he is said to have shouted, "Jerusalem, I love thee!"

If love is of Isaiah, it fits not Messalina. It is a poor banner indeed that serves the knight and the highwayman, and if it stands for crime and seduction, it does not grace issues sanctified by supreme devotion, loyalty, kinship and sacrifice.

LUST is lust and has its place, but not as a metaphysics.

M

MALEVOLENCE rides easily on the tongue; it is the good word that sets heavily in the throat.

MALICE is not innate but inbred.

MAN: Some love nature to the exclusion of man, but he is one of God's creatures, too.

*

Men are petrified children. If one would only try to visualize them as they were when children, one's understanding would be easier and one's judgment kindlier.

MANNERS: Man's toilette manners have improved, his church attitudes hardly changed.

*

Good manners may require restriction of conversation to pleasantries, but, then again, good manners will not improve the world.

MARRIAGE is the only business in which adolescents are permitted to make a contract.

MARXISM   created dictatorship over the proletariat, not by the proletariat.

MASSES: No man is so small that he does not consider himself above the masses.

*

They say the masses need religion; rather the power-mad leaders need it and need it badly.

*

The masses are not those who think but don't know; rather are they those who know but don't think.

MATERIALISM: I suspect the enemies of materialism. They either live off idealism or drape it about themselves like a cloak to keep from being touched by the tears and sweat of the victims of ideologies.

MEDALS: The noncombatant invariably winds up with the largest string of ribbons and medals.

MEDICAL FALLACIES: There is hardly a medical fallacy that was not at one time or another "standard treatment." Who knows which one of our present "standard treatments" will be the fallacy of tomorrow?

MEMORY: The power of remembering may be a gift, but the power to forget is a blessing.

＊

Why retain a mental picture of trifles? Only great events are worth remembering.

MERCY   is thrice justice.

MIDRASH   or the oral interpretation of the Bible has about run its full course and exhausted every possible aspect. We need less exegesis and more emphasis on the true principle of the Old Testament, which can be reduced to a one-page fundamental.

MIND: A glass splinter reflecting a ray of infinite Sun, dreaming of itself as hearth of the universe.

＊

Too much emphasis is given to the mentally deviated and not enough to the mentally corrupted. It is not the neurotics who retard the world's progress, but the ruthlessly ambitious.

＊

There are some ill-fitting gears in the mental machinery. To most questions we seem to find, or hope for, a corresponding answer, yet there are queries open that foil even an attempt to reply.

*

Mind mirrors reality, or only glows like a window reflecting a distant ray—who can fathom this phantom looking glass?

*

Mind measures the vastness of galaxies, visible and supposed, and finds it can not sustain the vision of endless firmament. Endless space and infinite time are just the whisper of a bewildered soul.

If God is anywhere, He dwells within that heart of hearts raising its eyes to the infinite. God finds Himself in the mind of man; the mind's vision of God is God Himself.

MIRACLE: Nothing seems to the masses more plausible than the improbable.

MINORITY: The student of history knows that the minority has, often as not, been closer to the truth than the dominant group.

*

A minority has no right to govern, but a claim to be respected.

MIRROR: Every once in a while we stop and

quickly glance at our friend to find out how we look in his eyes. The rest of the world matters little—it is how our friend reflects our deed that counts. We all live lonely lives except for that mirror.

MISMANAGEMENT openly acknowledged is a sign of democracy; in tyrannies there *seems* to be always perfection.

A MOB has many heads, but most often only one cunning brain doing its scheming.

MONUMENTS should be erected to the great evildoers. It is more important to keep them fresh in the public memory than the bene-factors.

MORALITY is the observance of the rights of others. One can not be immoral but in rela-tion to others. What one does to oneself or with oneself may be wise or foolish, but never immoral.

One may abuse his body and yet be respectful of the welfare of others and thus quite moral. And one may discipline his flesh with all precepts of hygiene and ascetism and be a hard, selfish, hurtful person and thus grossly immoral.

[90]

It is only in relation to society that man is good or bad, moral or immoral. By himself he may be sober and moderate or very careless, but never good or bad.

*

I do not think that abstinence is a way to morality, but goodness is.

*

Morality is always the same. However, immorality varies from generation to generation.

*

Nothing is immoral that is not meant to hurt others, and nothing is moral that is meant to do so.

MUSIC: The wordless cry of the inner soul reaching for love's fulfillment and beatitude. Beethoven's symphonies, the slow movements: The Lord Himself walks through the silent forests of His domain.

*

There is another music: the stirring beats of lusty savages, the screech and fury of bored sophisticates jazzing a tired night to death, the whinny of the devil on the brink of borderline humanity.

[91]

I have often wondered why men write music to poetry and rarely poetry to music. It would be a great and new art to set the symphonies of Beethoven into poetry!

N

NAMES should be changed to suit men. Some
trail ludicrous appendages after them. I have
seen giants with names suitable for a dwarf
and women with men's names.

*

Names should be means of identification
and decoration, not embarrassment and confusion.

NASTINESS is the tyranny of the peewee.

NATIONALISM: It is peculiar that national-
istic zealots are not even natives of the countries they allegedly wish to glorify: Alexan-
der was not a Greek, Napoleon not a Frenchman, Hitler not a German, and Stalin not a
Russian.

THE NATURALIST examines the hem of God
and he thinks he feels the pulse of the Lord.

NATURE: Who can fathom why nature is so

designed that creatures can exist only by destroying other creatures?

❊

Nature, never wrong, wrongs many.

NEGRO: Someday a lotion may solve an issue where emotion failed; a yet-to-be-found chemical will neutralize the dark pigment of our neighbors and leave the many palefaced inferiority complexes stranded on their prejudices.

NEGRO BAITERS: They call on Jesus in the church and on Beelzebub in the street.

NEIGHBORS: One always carries their picture with him, but often it is a caricature.

Do not bother loving them—just cease hating them.

NEUROTICS: The American society is hard on the hunt for neurotics, but the great evils in the world are perpetrated by the so-called normals, not the deviates.

In Russia, sober, calculating politicians are keeping millions in concentration camps and are giving a deadly time to their Jewish citizens, for instance, simply in an opportunistic speculation of gaining power in Western

[94]

Asia. In Red China scores of educators and jurists, following a peculiar brand of socialism, advise the young on how to denounce their parents who do not follow the official party line. Such denouncements invariably end with the elders being publicly executed before the very eyes of grisly, elated, icy youth.

And in our lands, cold-eyed townsmen of the South refuse to convict perpetrators of murder and kidnaping on blacks, while unemotional, shrewd legislators of the White Council stamp rant against basic principles of humanity.

All these and many other sinister elements in our society are the drags that stop humanity from rising to loftier heights, not the unimportant neurotics screwed up in their petty little complexes.

NEUTRALISM: In the fight between the red and the black, some prefer to remain colorless. If you look hard you may note the yellow showing through.

NEW ERA: A new epoch began with the Nuclear Terror overhanging. We have left the era of incessant wars and entered the period of peaceful animosity.

NEWS is not what you read today but what happened today.

NOBILITY: The psychoanalyst wants you to do the smart thing, God wants you to do the noble thing. Where do you wish to make your place, on the couch or in history?

❋

Nimbus rises not from a calloused palm or a belabored brain, but from a gentle heart.

❋

Many have searched for the causes of evil-doing in man, but the answer to the riddle of the nature of man lies in the origin of human nobility.

O

OBEDIENCE   to the rule of the tyrant is nothing but rationalization by the moral slave.

OLD AGE: Stars that have been ignored all morning, noon and evening open up in the late of the night to brighten the hours of the lonely wakeful.

OPINION: The great obstacle to truth is the common man's lethargic reluctance to make a thorough house-cleaning of his mind.

OPPORTUNISM: There are two ways of looking at the world and there are two ways of leading one's life: to do what is right, or to do what is opportune. By this proposition there are two types of persons, opportunists and the right kind of people.

✤

How many rush to the support of the strong when the weak are in distress!

OPTIMISM can be a matter of philosophy as well as disposition.

ORATOR: Being great in rhetoric without profound calling or message is like being adept in stage fencing—without purpose or honor to the rapier.

ORATORY: The magic quality of making a trickle thunder like a torrent.

ORTHODOXY: No one is more insufferable on rigidity of observance than the man who has nothing else.

*

Orthodoxy with many is purely pretentious or nostalgic, like the meat-eater belonging to a vegetarian society.

OTHERS: What makes you think you look better to others than they look to you?

OUR WORLD: God is in His heaven and the Devil on earth.

OVERLORDSHIP was once established by the strong fist, then by the keen blade, and now by the sharp tongue.

P

PAIN: The gentlest balm is lost on those who suffered no pain.

*

Pain is most often self-inflicted.

PASSING: You shall not live your years again, so treasure them hour by hour.

PASSION is given to prophets as well as to sinners.

PAST: Our known past is but a brief paragraph in the book of time.

PATRIOTISM: So many of the great patriots were and are men of age. Men whose life is flowing away caress the beloved nation of which they are a part. It is in the love of his people that mortal man never dies.

*

Patriotism is too often not an attitude but a profession.

*

The patriot is not the one who loudly

praises his own; he is just a braggart. A patriot is the man who praises the land and the people that are dedicated to freedom and brotherhood.

PEACE with the devil remains a one-sided arrangement.

✿

Even an angel could not live in sanctity with the Devil about.

PENS: Too many push a pen who should wield a broom.

PEOPLE: Whoever loves not his people, loves not God. The Lord made the covenant with a nation, not an individual.

✿

Perhaps the people are as gullible as the charlatans seem to prove.

✿

You can't remake all people, but you can manage to avoid some of them.

✿

The voice of the people is seldom their own.

PERFECTION: The perfect man is not one without faults, rather, one burdened with all

[100]

sins and blessed with the will to overcome them.

PETS: So long as there is a suffering waif starving in this bitter world it is a sin to cater to a dog.

PHILANTHROPY: Those who criticize charity are only bothered by a bad conscience.

*

Watching public benefactors is an embarrassment to the indifferent; they will steadfastly belittle the motives of the donors, having themselves no motive at all.

PHILISTINES: They give such little answers to such big questions.

PHILOSOPHERS: The world is full of peacock philosophers who forever are preoccupied with their own feathers.

PHILOSOPHY can never be defined because it is the search for the indefinable.

*

All man's world is in man's mind; man's mind *is* man's world.

To the timeless universe coursing through infinite space, what is all this but the dreams and doodlings of a blade of grass in the evening wind?

That which man calls "beauty"—what is it? That which man calls "moral"—what is it? What he calls "heritage"—what is it? The blade of grass is singing in the wind and it thinks the wide, wide universe hearkens.

Man must still live as if his world were real and perennial, but if he finds his true and tiny measure, a better man he may be—more humble, more kind, more forgiving, more hesitant.

✻

Hesitance is the beginning of philosophy, and charity its end.

✻

It is the ability to hesitate before forming an opinion that makes the difference between a philosopher and, shall we say, a parroty mind. Snap judgments are like fishing nets cast with great flourish and prematurely hauled in. A lot of seaweed and broken shell may come up, but hardly any fish.

✻

Philosophy is either a way of life or just a figure of speech.

PITY   is where man meets God in fellow man.

PLEASANT: There is nothing more irritating than unpleasant things said in a pleasant manner.

PLEASURES   can be found where you least expect them.

POETRY: Language of the wounded soul.

❋

Whispering melody from the faraway shores or man's pained soul, true poetry is ever melancholy. Plato named it a mania. Is that why every fifth one of the great bards lived or died in broken mind?

POLITICS: A profession holding out the greatest amount of power for the least amount of training or responsibility.

POSTERITY: Let's not hope for a better tomorrow, but better our today.

POTENTATES: The world has always had those who take on the voice of God, and sound off for themselves—those with the cunning tongues who, in depicting the Lord's celestial abode, never fail to point out their

own right of eminent domain in its ante-
room.

POVERTY is the disgraceful symptom of our
whole known era, that forever wastes the
people's sweat on the mansions of the rulers,
cheapens the price of blood in defense of
them, and raises the cost of bread for the
expendables.

Only the freedom of tears exists among
the masses of Eurasia and Africa. And the
princes of Arabia or India, the chieftains of
Russia or China, may toss a fortune into arm-
lets or arms while the people perish in want
of nourishment.

POWER still comes first in Eurasia's nations,
with scholarship a stumbling, rationalizing
second. After the ugly deed is done, theory
is called in to contrive justification.

PRAISE houses in one den with slander.

PRAYER: Where the heart does not long for
love eternal and peace among men there is
no communication with the Divine; there is
no true prayer. Prayer is the pining of the
soul of man for the soul eternal, in this aim-

lessly drifting world of evil and illness, pain and deceit.

✿

Those who pray to God for blessings beggar the grace of worship.

✿

A serene word, a chapel on your lips, if those lips were only for fellow man and fellowship instead of for favors and privileges for the personal flesh.

✿

With the slaughter, in less than a decade, of every third Jew by the German people, in the souls of worshipping Jews Divine Providence receded into the background. The mood of the Synagogal worshipper changed from the prayerful to the meditative. Judaism, especially Reform Judaism, shifted to a philosophical vein: God no longer benevolent father, but *ens perfectissimum*, the light of cosmic cognition, *Or Adonai*.

✿

The Lords knows your needs, what wants revealing are your deeds.

✿

Pray to your conscience for guidance and not to the Lord for deliverance.

[105]

PREJUDICE: Logic is ever so often the handmaiden of prejudice.

*

Nothing is better established than prejudice, hatefulness and superstition, and nothing sounds more convincing than an old lie.

*

The prejudiced will only know what his
fellow man lacks, not what he possesses.

*

Superstitions and prejudices of distant
lands and times are readily apparent. It is
those close by that are difficult to discern.

*

Its practitioner is a usurer hiding the inter-
est. He pleads high principles but only poorly conceals his personal advantage.

PREACHING is like delivering an ambassadorial
message: it is the king's voice that should
prevail and not the messenger's fancy.

THE PRESS   should be free but not loose.

PRIDE   is a virtue if it is the measure of one's
own nobility. It renders itself a sin when its
intent is to make others appear ignoble.

PRISONS: There must be a better way of re-

educating offenders than herding them like
unruly cattle into a pen.

PROGRESS: In the last five thousand years we
have been going two steps forward and three
steps backward.

*

Tribes used to call each other by beating
on tree trunks, then by scratching on clay
tablets and paper, and now via electrons.
Still, after thousands and thousands of
years, the text of the messages has not
changed: tribe trafficking with tribe to destroy other tribes.

PROOF: You can't prove anything where inter-
est dominates reason.

PROPERTY: Because fortune attaches itself to
a man does not make him a fortune hunter.

THE PROPHET   knows no more than ordinary
man but he knows it earlier.

*

Very few, blessed few, pin their faith di-
rectly on the hem of God. Most ordinary
people anchor their beliefs in other mortals
who link God to them. The Hebrews called
these prophets *nebiim,* "interpreters."

PROSPERITY   is as often the midwife of generosity as of arrogance.

PROVERBS: Much cherished wisdom of Western philosophers was, millennia before, folk
wisdom in other continents.

*

Proverbs are the mirror of a people. If we
read the proverbs of the Sumerians or Isra-
elites, ancient as the sands of the desert, we
begin to realize how little we have added in
all the thousands of years to their wisdom of
life.

PROVIDENCE is childishly anthropocentric
wish-thinking that the Sun will change
course to blow a dust particle off a petal.

THE PRUDE is closer to sin than the indifferent,
in fact, the former is ever on the brink of it.

PRUDENCE may fill the purse but empty the
heart.

PSYCHOANALYSIS: The attempt to cure ab-
errations of the present by recalling aber-
rations of the past.

*

Mind bespeaks itself. One who finds his
milieu a forest of sexual symbols reveals

more the status of his own brain than that of his environs.

✿

Psychoanalysis has added many new words to our language but no new insights.

✿

Dreams are the play of a drowsy mind; only fools and children take a game for real.

PSYCHOSOMATICS: Many illnesses originate in the mind; the body lives correspondingly. The problem is: which came first, the inside of the shell or the outside?

PUNISHMENT is not the answer to the problems of crime; it answers only the call for revenge.

Q

QUESTIONS: A thousand questions can be posed off the beaten path; even correct replies will lead nowhere.

R

THE RABBI speaks of the Sages and the Sages speak of God. You cannot place a statue on the bare ground, you need a pedestal. The rabbis are the pedestal. It is a thankless lot to have chosen. They serve to enhance the greatness of the Masters and the best they get is to be overlooked.

RACE: God cannot see the marks and markings by which humans distinguish themselves from others. He can but see the humans.

*

A thousand things distinguish man from man, but only one distinguishes man before God—his conscience.

*

Little people make much of the little which makes them different from another, but to the aeons eternalizing the universe, man differs from man as barely as a dust grain varies from a dust grain.

How little do we know of man's past and how much do we make of that little we know.

*

Race is good when taken as an obligation, evil when taken as a privilege.

*

If each race were human, there would be only one.

REASON: The semblance of reason is often more attractive than reason itself.

REFORM is seldom effective without a dose of reaction.

REPUTATION is not worth defending, but righteousness is.

RESIGNATION: Perhaps the wisest begin and end their lives in obscurity, and even in passing, steal away from the rest without an epitaph—unknown giants in a realm of dwarfs.

RESURRECTION: The breathtaking concept of man's religion, an immortal soul in eternity! —in small eyes, a selfish vision of personal reward in a comfortable hereafter arranged by a police-judge type deity for the goody-goodies.

REVIEWERS: Some forget that they are only heralds and not the hero of the play.

RIGHT may not always make might, but you'll not find it on your knees.

*

The test of existing rights lies in daily practice, not in abstract constitutions.

RIGHTEOUSNESS: It is never too late to start on the path of righteousness, and the road to evil will always be only a step away.

ROMANCE lives not in the people but in their dreams. Who does not dream will never encounter the greatness of love, daring, adventure, and devotion.

ROYALTY: Somewhere on every royal coat of arms should be engraved an executioner's axe.

*

Royalty used to carry a scepter, now a vodka bottle.

S

SABBATH is not sanctified by abstention from work, but rather by devotional attention.

SALVATION: Socrates has no followers because his testament was that salvation must be earned by every man for himself. Jesus' flock runs into millions because he took the pains of salvation upon himself.

SANCTITY OF LIFE is a great principle to uphold but greater yet is that of the dignity of man.

*

Sanctity of life is a noble but inconsequential attitude. The ankle bell of the Hindu, which sends out warning to whatever crawls of the crushing threat of his feet, sounds gentle enough, but besides the millions of ticks and worms that draw their life from the skin and blood of man, there are billions of minutely tiny beasts infesting man's arteries and tissues that must be poisoned so man may live. Holy only is the life of no sin; much of the animal life that crawls and flies is a curse to man and a disease.

SCHOOL: Youth has a right to be regarded as a goal and not as a means. In free society every boy and every girl has a right to live a young life of self-respect and respect without comparison to others, be they better or worse, more clever and adept or less cunning and diligent. If a teacher can not deal with the young but by the whip of threats and the bribe of rewards, he is as little fit to sit under the blackboard as a judge with such a frame of mind would be fit to sit on the bench.

Every boy and girl has a right to have his or her natural gifts of body and mind tended to, be they great or small, as individual talents, without being driven to demoralizing contests for scholastic rewards, without being subjected to the dehumanizing effects of shabby victories over classmates and equally dehumanizing humiliation of alleged failure. It is easy to deal with pupils, whip in one hand and honey in the other. Labor used to be dealt with in the very same way, but the time has come to drop the sorry tradition of competitive schooling as the time came generations ago to drop the tradition of competitive labor management.

The praise and rewarding of the gifted and diligent is as demoralizing as the public criticism of the less endowed and less patient, because the goal of education does not lie in the subject, but rather in the student. It isn't what you put in the student that matters so much as what you bring out of him. You may pour into his brain with Nuremberg funnel all the seven wisdoms, up to the rim; if you can't get out of him the spark of human kindness and the yearning to raise the standards of mankind in a life of cooperation, you may have gained him a whole array of honors and medals, but you have rendered no service to youth and society.

❈

School is the place where family prejudices are replaced by public ones.

SCIENCE: Man's ax got sharper, not his wit.

❈

Knowledge makes man neither free nor good. The Romans, most learned of ancient

[116]

peoples, tolerated Caligula and Nero, and enthusiastically carried the scourge of the Fasces into peaceful neighboring lands. The Germans, most learned of the twentieth century, elected a paranoiac housepainter as chancellor and tumbled gleefully from executions to death-camps and back.

Knowledge and science are tools that can be used for evil as readily as for the good. The scientist or scholar is not made a better man by his knowledge, only a more dangerous one.

*

Perhaps science has harnessed enough of the powers of nature; let us now harness the powers of science.

*

Science began with a gadget and a trick. The gadget was the wheel; the trick was fire. We have come a long way from the two-wheel cart to the round-the-world transport plane, or from the sparking flint to man-made nuclear fission. Yet I wonder whether the inhabitants of Hiroshima were more aware of the evolution of science than ancient man facing an on-storming battle chariot.

It isn't physics that will make this a better life, nor chemistry, nor sociology. Physics may be used to atom-bomb a nation and chemistry may be used to poison a city and sociology has been used to drive people and classes against classes. Science is only an instrument, no more than stick or fire or water that can be used to lean on or light or refresh, and also can be used to kill or burn or drown. Knowledge without morals is a beast on the loose.

*

Science is hidden behind a tight web. Every so often someone unravels a tiny thread, getting a glimpse into her mysteries. A thousand riddles are still far away from our peepholes.

*

They teach what science has accomplished. They need to tell also, and more so, the unfinished business of science, the long index of matters unknown and problems unsolved.

SECOND CHILDHOOD: The old seem to be in second childhood because they have learned that much of life is better taken as a game than a battle.

[118]

bondsmen, and kidnaped blacks by Christians.

The freeing of slaves, tragically enough, was not done by, but in spite of, the Church.

SLEEP is a refueling process of body and mind. Sleepers' chill is indicative of the great energies used in this process. Perhaps some day a way will be found to replace the natural manner of slumber's revitalization by speedy chemical means. The Man of Tomorrow may not sleep at all.

*

Perhaps it is Sleep that, in replenishing the body energies, saps our strength. Is that why they call him the brother of Death?

SMILE: A smile is still the best make-up for a face.

*

The flag of truce in a world of strife.

*

The manner of wisdom.

*

Smile! If only for the lift it gives your company.

SNOBBERY is an attitude of infantile forgetfulness—forgetfulness that in this fleeting ocean

[122]

SECURITY is a blessing, but not if bought at the expense of fellow man.

SELF-GOVERNMENT: Perhaps some of the less modern nations do not yet know how to govern themselves, but their colonial masters have certainly proven they can not do it for them.

SELF-IMPROVEMENT is a meaningless effort. The Self is God-given and wants no betterment. The task is to reach one's Self and to be true to it conscientiously.

SELFISH: All men are selfish, but how their selves differ!

SELF-KNOWLEDGE: Everyone knows himself best, but refuses to admit it for fear of incrimination.

SENTIMENTAL: People sometimes forget the object of their feelings for the atmosphere about them.

SERENITY is as often the result of indifference as it is the sequel to philosophy.

SERMON: The flocks should leave impressed by the Lord, not by the Rabbi.

[119]

SERVILITY   is a form of inverted arrogance.

*

Those who bow to the man above will always step on the man below.

SEX   was always here but never so much talked about.

*

If it were man's dominant motive, then the peasant who conducts his sex life on the level of stable husbandry could be considered its best adjusted master.

SHREWDNESS: Experience makes for shrewdness; it's the heart that makes for wisdom.

SILENCE   may be golden, but sometimes it is only yellow.

*

Silence is the voice of the convinced; loudness is the voice of those who want to convince themselves.

*

It is not the stillness of the tongue that matters but the silence of the heart.

SIMPLICITY: The truly wise are always simple. It is the little mind that spins complications.

SIN   is sweet. Were it not, it would not be necessary to prohibit it.

Sin is the weak man's failing, man's secret.

SINNERS   lead an interesting life but with loss of their capital.

SKEPTICISM   is only an approach to s not wisdom itself.

SKY   is just an ocean of gases in which tr of minute creatures are floating; they s around the tasty globe like gnats arou cut fruit, these ubiquitous tiny beasts, inf ing man, animal and plant.

SLAVERY: It is shocking that the two philos phers who dominated the Western mind fc two thousand years, Plato and Aristotle, up held slavery as a God-given institution.

Slavery was certainly not born with Plato and Aristotle. But both these men justified, to an adulating Europe of so-called Christian faith, the idea that some were born free and some born slaves.

The fantastic situation lies in the utter indifference of the Christian world to the obvious contradictions existing between the teachings of Christ about the equality of men and the prevalent enslavement of serfs,

of life all these man-made distinctions born of petty desire, created by smallish minds, are mere pebbles over which the water-mountains float endlessly, majestically.

❖

You can't pull rank on God. No man walks past Saint Peter's gate with a monocle in his face.

SOCIALISM: The blueprint of paradise over a foundation of purgatory.

❖

A government of the many at the mercy of a few.

❖

The shamefaced cousin of communism, losing virtue by kinship rather than misdeed.

❖

SOLITUDE is a state of mind, not a geographic position. There are no lonelier places than certain spots in certain crowds.

SOPHISTICATE: A person who derides all standards in order to avoid the job of studying them.

❖

Wisdom by necessity will "no" some things and "yes" others; the frivolous steal the nimbus of wisdom by deriding all and sundry.

SORROW is the messenger of friendship.

SOUL: People show more care in choosing a repair man for their car than one for their soul.

SPACE TRAVEL: We are morally in no better position attempting to visit other planets than the murderous goldhunters Cortez and Pizarro. We are a nefarious lot with a record of twenty million killings in the last few decades alone. What have we to offer? A globe that has not learned in a million years to govern itself and still feels ready to strike out for new territory.

SPEECH: Don't judge a man until you have heard him speak. The voice is the truest mirror of mind and intent.

SPIRIT is the spice of life. It is *Shechinah*, the Hebrew for the living God. Of course one can live a whole existence on a spiceless diet.

STAFF OF LIFE: A man's soul feeds on either love or hate. Some live on the pleasures of the good deed; others are of such disposition that only doing hurt and harm will nourish them. Ormuzd and Ahriman, Moses and Pharaoh. . . .

So many live on a diet of hate, cherishing

envy and greed like satiating herbs, while love is shunned like a poison. These cannibals of the soul have infested the caves, tents, and roofs of all the continents. They have made man cry out in anguish of war and torment since the birth of Adam.

But somehow there always rose those who would bear the symbols of the Lord and stretch out their arms in beatitude.

STATESMAN: The path of the statesman is haunted by politicians—starlings in the flight of the eagle.

*

Statesmen see themselves as handmaidens of history; politicians see the state as a handmaiden of themselves.

STUPIDITY is sometimes more of a defense than a characteristic.

STYLE: Mind makes the style, not vice versa.

SUB-HUMAN: Some are wizened by human affairs, others by sub-human.

SUCCESS: I know of no greater failure than the man who devotes his life to the achievement of success.

*

The man who sets success as his goal is

doomed to failure, since one desire for achievement succeeds another in the endless chain of human vanity.

SUICIDE: To die at one's own hand may be of more grace than living in subjugation or disease.

THE SUN: It is not earth that is mother of man, but the sun. The sun gives its nourishing rays of the plants, which man and his animal-food live on; the sun evaporates the water that filters into man's springs; the sun warms the air man breathes and the ground he walks on. Man is truly a child of the sun. Still, whence does Helion draw its matter and energy? Wherefrom the unknown and perhaps peregrine donor?

*

The energies that carry this our globe and billions like it through space and time are breath-taking. And this is but the tiny universe that our tiny cornea envisions.

What mysterious other attributes must that Unknown Eternal possess that we call with the ancient nomen: God. Perhaps the Hebrews were right in warning: Name it naught but the Eternal, the One.

[126]

The Sun is what you make it—the Light of Lights or just an extension of bursting gases.

SUPERIORITY: There are no people with a superiority feeling, only those with an uncontrolled desire to hide their inferiority.

SUPERSTITION is the ante-room to religion where those remain who cannot get an audience with their own selves.

SUSPICION may as well be the gate to knowledge as to hate.

SUTTEE: The now obsolete Hindu practice of burning widows exmplifies the petrification of moral principles. In later scriptures of Hinduism there is a solemn plea for connubial devotion beyond the grave.

T

TALE: Truth is so hard to tell, it sometimes needs fiction to make it plausible.

TALK: Deep-bottomed boats travel slowly.

❋

Talk is primarily a way of killing time. Perhaps that explains its popularity.

❋

Mankind divides itself into two types: dialogue people and monologue people. The latter never hear you or your side since they are pauseless monologists.

❋

A peasant may be more interesting than a scholar if the peasant opens his soul and the scholar only an odd book.

❋

Though you don't hear the fish, it doesn't mean they are not talking.

❋

Some talk of a thousand different things

and still speak only about themselves.

TASTE   is the feeler of man's appetite and still the best judge of right nutrition.

&

Taste is spoiled in childhood by parental prejudice and in adults by customs and fads.

TEARS   come readily from shallow souls.

TELEOLOGY: Man is as little the final purpose of divine providence as an elk or a beetle or a salamander.

&

Teleology in its attempt to find a man-suiting purpose in nature will have to contend with the teleology of plants, animals and perhaps other entities.

Were the sunflowers placed in the meadow as supply source for the bees; or as food for some parasites; or for man to look at; or to drop to the ground and serve as fertilizer for surrounding weeds?

What a tragicomic pose! Tiny man no bigger than a mold travelling on a gigantic rock through billions of years and miles in an unfathomed galaxy of innumerable worlds, yet hollering at the top of his inaudible voice: Hear me, trillions of universes, aeons

[129]

of times, infinities of space! I, man, earth-bound fungus, 98 per cent water, 2 per cent phosphor and such, I am the aim and end of it all. I am the purpose of all this majestic movement in its mysterious history!

Perhaps the Torah was right in forbidding man to set himself in stone or paint, lest he feel himself lasting or even everlasting. Is he more than a pinch of dust with a whisper of breath?

❊

If there be purpose to this world in its crazy meandering, it can't be a good one. By all human reckoning there is more sin harvested in a day than goodness planted in a year. Man's inhumanity to man is vile in maturity; kindness is rare but always green.

TEMPER: Let your thoughts be burning, but your words cool.

TEMPTATION: The Devil just testing.

❊

It is easy to resist the big ones; the little ones cause havoc.

THINKING: The beginning of true thinking is silence.

❊

Thought is a twig on the tree of emotion

and instinct. As it was a million years ago, the first is still an outgrowth of the latter.

*

Men think quite alike; if it were different, they could not co-exist even for a day. But most people judge by traditional or imitated judgment patterns, and snap judgments are the rule and the rulers.

*

Is thinking ever free? Wherever I meet it, I find it chained to a *motive* of one kind or another. The world operates on motivated thinking tied to prejudice, opportunism, greed, narrow-mindedness, selfishness, and a thousand other little passions and passionettes that clutter up the narrow path of righteousness.

*

Thinking can be colored by heart, gall, glands, stomach, or even shifting eyes. Sometimes I wish that people's thoughts came in colors so one could see what part of the body sent them forth.

*

Thinking may be classified on a color chart, however, of poetic imagination. Some people's cogitations run rosy; others gray, even black. There are those who think yellow and those who live and breathe blood red. The minds of others are of peculiar color combinations. And there are sages whose badge is white, embodying all the colors. No human emotion is strange to them, yet none colors their thoughts.

❀

A good thought, even when poorly presented, will finally emerge right side up.

❀

The last thought is always wiser than the first.

TIME does not heal wounds, it just hides some and deepens others.

❀

How quickly does today turn into yesterday.

❀

Time took the wrong road. The Past was not all glory; there was wilderness. But now we are trapped in a Death Valley with no sight of a Tomorrow.

TOLERANCE appears in two editions, one bound in wisdom and one in indifference.

[132]

Tolerance is ill used on friends of the great sinners. When the sinners fall, some of their friends plead the thin excuse of compulsion. The sycophants are always ready to serve the new master and renounce the old, but the Hebrews said you can not be Abaddon, angel of the bottomless pit, and Gabriel in one person.

TOMBSTONE: Better study your epitaph now lest your tombstone belie its dead.

TOMORROW: If a tomorrow were never to come, it would not be worth living today.

TONGUE: The tongue is man's best friend but also his worst enemy.

*

The pen may be mightier than the sword, but mightier yet is the tongue. The tongue-waggers are the masters of our era, the Hitlers, the Stalins, the Mussolinis. The swish of their tongues is deadlier than all weapons.

*

Buddhists attribute four evils to the tongue —and only three to the rest of the body: slander, lying, idle talk and offensive speech. By their words you shall judge them. Vicious tongues have incited to world-wide massacre and have ever so much prejudiced thinking among men and nations, races and creeds.

TORTURE: Nature is beset with suffering, but of all beasts, only man makes a business of prolonging it.

TOTALITARIANISM: This granite earth we live on could be a bed of roses were it not for the scheming Procrustes and his fellow henchmen, be their shirts black, brown or red.

*

The Red camarilla has taken the romance out of socialism and replaced it with opportunistic expedience, thus losing the best of the idea and acquiring the worst that is in imperialist government.

TRAINING: You cannot train a horse with shouts and expect it to obey a whisper.

TRAVEL: People travel to faraway places to watch, in fascination, the kind of people they ignore at home.

THE TREE is the symbol of wisdom: it never shouts, and only whispers when it's moved.

TRUST is an expectation based more on the

hopes of the person having it than on the nature of the one trusted. No one is so deceitful that he has not been trusted by some and sundry.

TRUTH: How come the sages of all times speak the same truth? The Hebrews revere *Shalshelet Ha Cabbalah*, the Chain of Tradition. There is a chain of tradition running from the days of Ur to our time, but familiarity with the so oft-repeated pronouncements of the prophets has estranged us. Perhaps the sayings of our fathers should be translated into a foreign idiom and then brought back as a rare find, in order to be listened to again!

*

Man's mind is confounded by the deceitful twins: hearsay and gainsay.

*

Truth drops its wings before a low-ceilinged mind.

*

Truth hurts only the liar.

*

Truth may not make you free but falsehood will enslave you.

U

UGLINESS: Little uglinesses fill the air of our society like insects. They don't kill you, but they make life miserable.

*

Ugly faces suffer little temptation.

UNDERSTANDING exists on infinite levels. A moth comprehends the candle light, so do a dog and a bird; an infant figures it out, so do savage and savant. There are infinite attributes to all manifestations of the universe and endless variations of conception.

UNIONISM in the political and social fields runs smoothly uphill from the individuals to the centralized top. From there on, the chances are, star persuaders will drag the whole lot into a downhill alley of their own ambitions.

UNIVERSE: We know there are rhythms in the cosmos but who keeps the beat and what is the score?

There is more mystery in the yolk of an egg than in a galaxy of planets, if we could only fathom it.

*

Universe is only the little cosmos we see with eye and telescope. Beyond the beyond is *Pantaverse*, the endless worlds of worlds —*Ain Soph*, the Cabbalists named it, the One Without End.

UNPLEASANTNESS: With some, it is just a way of giving themselves airs.

UTOPIA: No promise or hope of tomorrow's better world is worth the price of today's liberty.

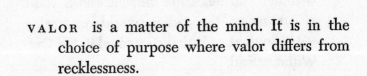

V

VALOR is a matter of the mind. It is in the choice of purpose where valor differs from recklessness.

VANITAS: If only the conquerers realized in time that their deeds are a game with worthless chips. After taking all the mountains and seas, they wind up like everybody else with a muddy slab of stone and their name on it.

VANITY can work through a display of poverty as well as through a show of wealth.

*

Vanity has no greater offender than the one who flaunts his indifference.

VEGETARIANS: Like the whale, they prefer flesh of the invisible animals to that of the visible ones.

VIRTUE carries its own reward. Were this not so, only the superstitious would pretend or seek it, anticipating post mortem advantages.

But true virtue, as well as true knowledge, is flavored by that rare beatitude called by the Hebrews *Simcha Shel Mitzwah,* "the pleasure of the right."

*

Beware the one whose virtue lies in the fear of God and not in the love of man.

*

All sins are common to all people, but virtue is of the few.

WAR is not in the nature of man; defense is.

❊

As far as the people themselves are concerned, they have little or nothing to gain by war, but everything—including their lives—to lose. In this sense, war is not in the nature of man, only in the nature of tyranny.

❊

Wars of independence are but the inverted will for peace.

❊

Perhaps the coming wars will be fought with pens instead of swords. The sting of the pen may be no less sharp than that of the edged weapon.

❊

Little men who want to be remembered start great wars; great men who wish to be forgotten are the architects of peace.

WAR MOGULS have forever prefaced their

military attacks with sanctimonious peace propaganda, accompanied by abuse of alleged warmongers.

WEAKNESSES: We see nothing clearer in others than our own weaknesses.

WEALTH of nations should be measured not only by the economy of material goods, but also by the resources in mind and heart. How poverty-stricken some of them are in their richness!

*

Wealth does not preclude virtue and poverty does not imply it.

WICKEDNESS harbors often within those you least suspect.

WILL riding the unbridled steed of passion thinks itself the master of the reins.

WISDOM: Any fool can see the fallacies of previous generations; to recognize those of his own takes great power of discernment.

*

There is a lot of foolishness in the wise and a lot of wisdom in the foolish.

Like victory, wisdom lies in the final out-
come, not in the individual contest.

WISHING is the hurdle on the track of thinking.

WOMAN is not an equal but rather a sequel to
man.

WOMEN so often confuse poseurs with pioneers.
The retinue of most charlatans is nine
women to one man, and about this one I am
not always sure.

*

Women are the bearers of culture but not
its makers. They read philosophy but do not
write it, play music but do not compose it,
view art and architecture but do not create
it.

WORDS spoken by sect-ridden prophets and
class-strugglers have done more to divide
people than issues or things themselves.

WORK is man's most natural form of relaxation.

WORLD: A chimaeric scheme of interconnect-
ing gears made up of living creatures who
can exist only by devouring each other.

WORSHIP is either Judaic or Pagan, philosophical or idolatrous. The Hebrews worship

no man, no saint, no priest, no face—only the *Echod,* the One, *Ain Soph,* the Infinite, *Elohim,* the Eternal.

The pagan, whatever his denomination, wants a man-god, a visible, walking, talking and personal god or goddess. He believes not in the invisible, he yearns for ikon and amulet, flesh and blood. But stone and flesh and blood and gold can not fix the heart of man to the *Or Adonai,* the light of the Lord, in which we see Him with our love and conscience, in deeds of justice and charity; which deeds are the Alpha and Omega of true faith.

*

Be familiar with the Lord. Invite Him as often to your house as you visit His.

WRITERS   are moved too much by the expectations of their public, rather than by their own momentum.

WRITING: Whoever writes with ease carries little weight.

*

So many with nothing to say keep on saying it.

Good writing is simple writing. Only confusion is complicated, truth never.

WRONGS: Were we to remember all wrongs done to us, we would live forever in hate.

*

A wrong forgotten is a wrong set right.

Y

YOUTH comes many times if the mind is kept aflow.

*

Youth is a state of mind.

Z

ZEAL: The Lord is not in want of zealots, but of souls.

ZEN: There are many shades of darkness, but only one principle of light. The experience of *Satori*, the enlightenment of Zen; the meditation into *Samahadi* of the Hindus; the *Tao* of Lao-tzu, the road to inner self—they all are only different symbols signifying the Hebraic *Or Adonai*, the light of God which Spinoza so beautifully named *Amor Dei Intellectualis*.

ZERO: They say that if all living humanity were placed body to body, they would fit into a cube no more than one mile in each dimension. One short mile out of the tens of thousands that make up this globe that, in turn, is just one battered rock out of billions of the kind we can see by eye and instrument.

Were one to visualize this one cubic mile of homo sapiens sunk into a canyon or crater, what becomes of the world and worlds? The blades of grass would rise green as ever, the waves of the seven seas would storm and heave, the lava never cease its flow in the volcano and the starry skies not even blink at the anthill of humans, all gone out at once instead of in bunches.

That cubic mile of man is destined for burial in some canyon or crater, all two and a half billion segments of it, within a few fleeting decades, but, dropping to the ground, they leave their offspring for a like existence of passing fortune, which gives them the feeling of perennial life.

If all people were to be buried on one day and in one casket, instead of in billions of small interments, perhaps that thought would make them realize how much like planetary dust their life, how ludicrous their arrogant distinctions of race, class and what they call religion, which means "binding," but with most of them serves rather to separate than unite.

Perhaps the day will come when this planetary dust that grew into flesh only to find its way back into a dugout of dust again, when this man of clay will truly reach awareness of his pitiful frailty and prove by deeds of charity and loving wisdom that somewhere, somehow in this mysterious universe there is a flame of godliness burning in aeonic distances and that a spark of this fire shimmers in the soul of man.

There is so little that we know even of what we can see about, beneath and above us, and what we can see is but a speck of the *Ain Soph,* the Endless, of which we can only dream in faint concepts.

Man's inhumanity to man has left its sanguine mark upon the earth and waters of this globe since the days of earliest recollection. Forever some cunning creature would rise in piracy upon his neighbors and sway his tribe to carry out a nefarious scheme of pillage, rape and conquest.

If only those strutting evil little masters of some anthill of land would understand that with all their bluster, medals and fanfare, they, too, are only clay on clay, and the dust of their graves is no respecter of tinsel and rank; and if the many who follow their power-usurpers on the bloody path of tyranny, if they, too, would learn it is better to lead a simple life on your feet than a fancy one on your knees.

If they would only understand that the pleasures of humiliating others and holding neighbors in chains are as fleeting as the dust in the wind—and that is all man is, dust in the wind of time.

If they would only understand that there is a serenity of the soul which comes with the practice of kindness to man, a serenity which outlasts the winds of time, since it is born in the heart of hearts, where dwells the insight into the majestic unity of this our universe.

You may call this God, or the voice of God; we Hebrews call it *Echod, Adonai, Elohim,* the One, the Lord, the Eternal.

Give it the name you will, this nameless One, but let your deeds be in His grace and His charity.